MY SUN RISES

Verses of Light and Shadow:
A Teen's Journey in Poetry

TRINITY

S.H.E. PUBLISHING, LLC

MY SUN RISES

Copyright © 2025 by TRINITY

For information contact: info@shepublishingllc.com
Website: www.shepublishingllc.com
Tel: 219.515.8032

Library of Congress Control Number: 2023952267

ISBN: 978-1-964061-25-2 *(paperback)*
Cover and Title Page Design by *Nabin Karna*

Amended First Edition: February 2025

10 9 8 7 6 5 4 3 2 1

TABLE OF CONTENTS

"Trinity's journey is one of growth and transformation. She is no stranger to hardship and pain, as well as to happiness and gain. In *My Sun Rises*, she captures the beauty of it all, sharing poetic stories based on her own experiences that uplift, empower, and inspire readers to discover their resilience and inner light, allowing their sun to rise and shine."

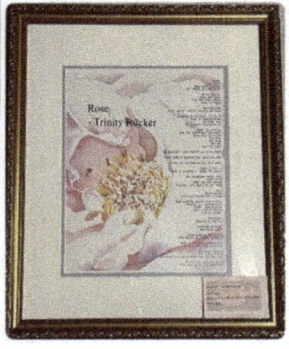

Being Us

By Trinity Rucker, City of Rockford's Youth Poet of 2024

Take a glimpse inside yourself.

Open your heart.

Search inside,
And find your spark.

Truly look within,
Search far and wide,
For your potential,
Despite when those bad thoughts come and subside.

Rise above the influence,
The sadness,
The hate.

Learn to love yourself and appreciate—
Tall, short, thick, thin.

Love the outside and within.

How could you love others
If you don't love yourself?

Don't ever lose your wealth.

Despite whom you've come to be,
There's always room to change,
To grow and amaze.

Room to fall,
But never stay down.

Know that the room shifts when you're around,
That you're an original,
The only you.

Fearfully and wonderfully made,
Know God promises it's true.

Come from pain to promise,
Death to life,
Leaving behind anger, jealousy, and strife.

Live life,
Being you,
The best you can be.

Life is but a blink of an eye,
So make history.

Speak life, not dead dreams.

Have no low self-esteem.

The cuts on your arm are from the past.

Put down the blade, the drugs, the guns,

And at last,
Love you for you,
Not who others want you to be.

Devil, get off of me.

We come to educate, elevate, and agitate,
People with our beauty,
Because we know that we are truly
One of a kind.

So, when you look in the mirror,
Also look inside.

See yourself for who you really are:
Not shameful,
Not broken,
But a star.

Discovery

By Trinity Rucker, City of Rockford's Youth Poet of 2024

A young girl carried around a heart full of sorrow.
Didn't even know if she would see tomorrow.

Tears fell every night;
She was filled with anger and strife.

Though she was loved, she couldn't see it.
Though she was loved, she couldn't believe it.

So she looked for happiness in temporary places.
People came and went,
So many faces.

She hated herself,
Couldn't see her wealth.

Couldn't see who she was meant to be,

Until one day, the devil had to flee.

A feeling overtook her—
Not something evil, but something that shook her.

Removed the covers from her eyes,
Removed the cuts from her thighs.

Removed the pain in her heart—
This was a new start.

No more broken bones,
No more houses, but homes.

No more heavy weights;
This "feeling" wiped her slate.

She'd heard about a man
Whom the mothers would praise,
Like something overtook them in a haze.

She'd heard about a man who changed lives,
That he would be the ultimate prize.

She'd heard about a man who sees us,
And his name was Jesus.

Real Love

By Trinity Rucker, City of Rockford's Youth Poet of 2024
Inspired for the YES (*Young Eagle Success*) Club

Real love is first learning to appreciate you,
Who you really are and what you've been through.

Real love is showing you care—
You don't have to search for it here and there.

Real love is standing side by side,
Smiling and not even knowing why.

Real love is a simple,
"How are you?"

Because, to someone, that question may be brand new.

We love because He first loved us,
In Him and His love we trust.

Real love carried inside our hearts—
Letting it flow out is when we have a start.

Unity in the CommUNITY

By Trinity Rucker, The City of Rockford's Youth Poet Laureate of 2024
S.H.E Publishing LLC's Award-Winning Poem

When you get the call three days before your birthday,
That your brother is gone,
Not out of town,
Not overseas,
But over the clouds
And trees.

All because the wrong person held a gun,
Clicked,
Pulled the trigger—
Now his life is done.

You don't cry at first,
Because you're only 10.
You suppose you have other things to worry about,
Not what had happened there and then.

But that's your brother.
How could you be so numb?
That's your family.

But what was done, was done.

One night, it hits you,
While you're sitting next to your bed,

That you have breath in your lungs,
And your brother is dead.

You cry out,
"Why, why him?"

Sobbing,
And the light seems so dim.

He was told the Lord would get him
So very soon—

Praying He would comfort family in their gloom.

Come, unity,
Why do you seem so far away?

I almost cannot see you in our community today.

One brother down,
How many left to go?

Almost too little on that Mother's Day, all those years ago.
Shot in the shoulder,
Left there to bleed.

I thank the Lord
In whom I believe.

Walking among us,
My brother's still here today.

If only we would stop the violence,
He's here to stay.

"I love Harpo, Lord knows I do,"
But it would be a miracle if someone didn't kill him dead.
A breakthrough.

Families getting torn apart
Each and every day.

Some blame the Lord—
How dare you?

When people are the problem, shooting children,
How could you think that's true?

When we wield the guns,
Waving them in people's faces,

Whose life can end the fastest?
Like it's some type of race.

And we joke about it when it's a disgrace.

Don't take for granted the breath that you have;
Someone's is gone with a single stab.

The pain in mothers' hearts,
When they see their baby's face on the news,

Then on a t-shirt,
Deep in the blues.

"Boo-hoo"—
You could make fun of the sob,
But drop the fake personality, the facade.

Don't mock pain you haven't been through,
How it consumed you daily and grew.

I have learned,
With a glimpse from the past,
That we need to drop the knives, the guns,
And at last—

Live amongst each other,
Coming, in unity,
Not beating and stabbing, brutality.

I can't stand seeing a new, dead face
On the news.
Can't stand knowing there's a baby out there who "goos,"
With an absent parent—
The pain is pretty transparent.

Can't witness the first word,
Steps,
What they do and don't like,

All because someone didn't know what to do with their anger and strife.

But when the gunpowder clears,
The truth of it all—

Is that we need to make a different call.

A call to action,
But not the violent kind—

A call of change,
One so divine.

I also have a dream
That we would all—

Embrace each other,
So the bodies wouldn't have to fall.

Thankfulness

By Trinity Rucker, City of Rockford's Youth Poet of 2024

I'm thankful for the hard times,
Times I didn't know if I would make it out,
Because the tears that I shed allowed my seed to sprout.

I'm grateful for the darkness,
Because I got to experience the light,
Experienced a worry-free life.

I'm thankful for the times I doubted myself,
Because when I pushed through, I discovered my wealth.

I'm thankful for the times of pain,
Because now it's easier for my joy to remain.

I appreciate the times I was hurt,
Because I was able to see beauty under all the dirt.

I'm thankful for forgiveness,
I'm thankful for being God's witness.

I'm thankful for each day that I'm given,
Both the easy and hard ones I'm livin'.

I'm grateful for the new experiences,
Finding out what "this" and "that" is.

I'm thankful for new faces,
New people and places.

I'm thankful for all the opportunities,
Grateful that I get to be a part of families.

Thankful for the trust that I've received,
I'm thankful for life's breeze.

I'm thankful for the ups and downs,
I'm grateful for the way the room shifts when I'm around.

I'm thankful for all the faces sharing it with me,
I'm thankful for all the gifts you give me,
I'm thankful for the way that you lift me.

My life is more than I could ask—
The present, the future, and the past.

Woman Impact

By Trinity Rucker, City of Rockford's Youth Poet of 2024

The women I grew up around were women of grace,
Not ones who talk behind your back and smile in your face.

The women I grew up around knew how to be strong,
They knew whatever suffering They endured wouldn't last long.

The women I grew up around,
weren't afraid to tell you what you needed to hear,
Even if it was painful, it still helped and was clear.

The women I grew up around carried your weight,
Shared the burdens you couldn't bear and didn't hesitate.

The women I grew up around inspired me,
Helped light a fire inside and instilled pride in me.

Held my head up
When things got tough,
Whispered in my ear that I was enough;
They never left me alone so that I got stuck.

It was God who put them in my life, not luck.

The women I grew up around are those of confidence,
Those who knew their worth and trusted in God's providence.

Because of these women, I've been able to endure.
Whatever I went through, they seemed to have a cure.

They are mothers, First Ladies, doctors, congresswomen, teachers, too.
Anything I could think of, they seem to do.

They help me remember and know that this true:
Friendships should be valued.
Cherish the ones you have,
Because anyone who finds a gem like that should be glad.

Me

By Trinity Rucker, City of Rockford's Youth Poet of 2024

This world of ours
Tries to mold us,
With the things that they've told us.

That we're
"Too big,"
Or
"Too small."

But we need to learn how to stand tall.

From the pimples
To dimples,

Thighs to our eyes,

Lips to our hips,
Even if we eat a lot of chips.

Our complexion is a connection to
Where we've come from.
But people are stressing when it's really a blessing—

To know who you are,

Not having to search far.

Being content,
Knowing what God meant.

Creating you,
Being fearfully and wonderfully made.

Not wanting to change yourself,
Not looking for a trade.

Learn to love yourself,
Learn your wealth,

And ask God if you need help.

My People

By Trinity Rucker, City of Rockford's Youth Poet of 2024

The world is filled with beauty,
Especially my people.
They take the pain from the past and soar like eagles.

You can't hold them down,
Can't hide them away.
No matter what, their beauty is on display.

From the texture of our hair,
To the sway of our hips,
To the care of our hands,
To the precious talk of our lips.

Our melanated skin glistens like gold,
Our extraordinary character could never be bought or sold.

My people's stories are passed down the line,
Educating and initiating with things so divine.

Through the haze of oppression, we found our way,
Seeking peace and harmony in every uncertain day.
We carry ourselves with grace,
Wrapped in God's embrace.

Our faith keeps us during times of trouble,
Because we know the joy will be double.

There's nothing we can't overcome,
No mountain we can't climb,
No barrier we can't break through in the nick of time.

With faith, we embrace our pain,
Because in life, lessons are learned and gained.

We stay true to ourselves,
Never losing our wealth.
We know the greatness we have inside—
It's so great that it cannot hide.

Because we're brave, and brilliant, and oh-so resilient.

We're fearfully and wonderfully made,
In every shape, size, and shade.
Our beauty never fades.

Our heritage is one of a kind,
It's God-given,
Divine.

Nothing compares to how we're there for each other,
And how we care for each other.

How we stand united, not divided,
Knowing that our love is not one-sided.

Because
It heals wounds and mends cuts,
Because we have each other, we have more than enough.

Our black is beautiful,
And it cannot be overthrown.

Our color is contagious,
And turns a house into a home.

Our ancestors breathe strength into the present day,
Our impact will never go away.

While our story is still being written,
And there's so much to say,
Let's celebrate what we have on today.

Unity

By Trinity Rucker, City of Rockford's Youth Poet of 2024
Inspired by the YES (*Young Eagle Success*) Club

As the Earth spins, so do we,
For we have many opportunities.
Stand hand in hand with smiles on our faces, showing love,
No matter what race.

Power of unity,
Fulfilled in our ecstasy.

The love of generations,
Passed all the way down to me.

From my mother and hers,
From your heart and words.

Sounds like 1 Peter 3:8 to me:
If we stand united, not divided,
Happiness will come, you see.

Freedom for one,
Freedom for all.
If we stand together,
We cannot fall.

We can withstand adversity,
Overcome tragedy.

When we have the audacity to
Cure the disease
Of racism, self-hate,
We need to come and clean the slate,

Opening that gate,
Walking into freedom,

And don't hesitate.

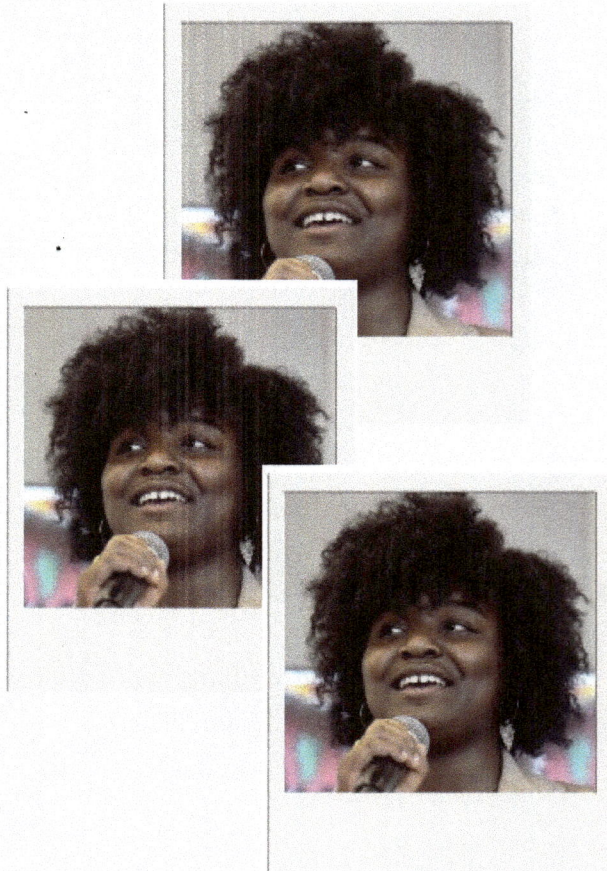

The Lord

By Trinity Rucker, City of Rockford's Youth Poet of 2024

Who created the sky?
Stretched out unique colors of blue.
And who created wonderful, beautiful you?
Who created the "perfect day"?
Blue sky,

Birds chirping,

Kids playing,

People singing,
And the church bells ringing?

Who created the beautiful sunset?
Reds, and pinks, and purples dashed across the sky.
The sun touching the ground, no longer up high.

Who allowed the day to come to an end?
Who made sure we would ascend?
Who placed the stars in the sky?

Leaving us to name them, never really knowing why.

But one I know for sure, so very clear:

Jesus Christ, my light and who is near.

He tucks me in at night,
' Makes sure I would sleep tight.
He woke me up this morning,
Blood still running through my veins.

Allowed me to breathe, now that a new day has come.
Made sure that every "I love you" was never in vain.
He was my umbrella when I was in the rain.

My Town

By Trinity Rucker, City of Rockford's Youth Poet of 2024

Walking through my hometown,
Seeing images that look just like me.

Reds, blues, and pinks,
But behind them is someone's story.

Capturing the beauty of the future,
If we just wait,

Loving as we anticipate.

Embracing our town,
And the people within.

Different lives that we are livin',

Children
Of all different races,
Being able to hold smiles on their faces.

People,
Both young and old,
All have something beautiful to hold.

Walking into a bright future with the lessons from the past,
Walking in together,
With unity,
At last.

Years, No More Tears

By Trinity Rucker, City of Rockford's Youth Poet of 2024

Years and years of being outcasts,
Years and years of being viewed as a threat,
Years and years of being looked down on,
Years and years of being the white man's pet.
Years and years of getting zero respect.

"We're all equal."
Who is "we"?
I'm not you. No, I don't have blue eyes and blonde hair.
Every time I walk into a room, people stop and stare.
Is my melanated skin a crime,
Or does it make me worth a dime?

Exchanging my people for a pretty penny,
Tearing apart families and shattering many.
Despite these things,
We will still rise—
Flying, then soaring,
Disregarding the lies.

Black is beautiful,
Both you and I.
We will rise,
Fought the good fight,

Both day and night.
The march,
The boycott,
Until the inequality stopped.

The time is now—
Yes, it is here,
To put an end to those years and years.
Years and years of being outcasts,
Years and years of being viewed as a threat,
Yes, years and years of being looked down on,
But no more being the white man's pet,
For we all deserve respect.

Years and Years

By Trinity Rucker, City of Rockford's Youth Poet of 2024

Years and years of being outcasts,
Years and years of being viewed as a threat,
Years and years of being looked down on,
Years and years of being the white man's pet,
Years and years of getting zero respect.

"We're all equal."
Who is "we"?
I'm not you. No, I don't have blue eyes and blonde hair.
Every time I walk into a room, people stop and stare.
Is my melanated skin a crime?
Or does it make me worth a dime?

My hair might not be straight and blonde, but it's valid.
Who are you to determine what I can and can't do?
"We're equal," you say.
Then why are my people being beaten until they draw their last breath?
Why does it not matter when a Black family has a death?
Why are we getting zero respect?

Harriet Tubman, Martin Luther King Jr., Ruby Bridges, and more—
All their efforts, yet we're still treated poor.

When?

When will it stop?
When will you take your blue eyes and blonde hair and realize that you don't
have to stop and stare?
When will you realize that I'm a person too, that I'm not a threat to you?
I shouldn't be seen as a Black girl.
I should be seen for what I am: a person.
Not an object,
Not a maid,
Not a criminal,
Not a punching bag,
But a human.

Black History,
His story,
Our story.
We live on, hardly getting glory.
We fight just to survive because we don't have blue eyes and blonde hair.

Why?
Why must we fight?
Why must we fear for our lives while walking the streets, day or night?

Whipped and whipped,
My ancestors have stripes on their backs.
Every day, they were under attack.
Centuries later, and we're still being beaten,
Police officers bringing us to our knees.
"No freedom until we're equal."
I guess freedom will never come.
Run through the Underground Railroad,
Run from the cops,
It seems like the run will never stop.

Melanin is not a crime.
How hard is that to understand?
Punishing me because of a curly hair strand? Because I'm different?

Why?
Why can't you just let my melanated skin shine?
Why?

After years and years of beating us until our hearts beat one last time,
Years and years of you walking all over us,
Years and years of you seeing us as animals, something you don't believe
deserves respect,
Years and years of putting my people through misery,

Why?
For power?
Glory?
Or because you just don't like that I'm different from you and breathing?

Yes, I Can!

By Trinity Rucker, City of Rockford's Youth Poet of 2024
Inspired by the YES (*Young Eagle Success*) Club

I believe and receive
The promise that is.

I can do all things
Through Christ who strengthens me.

When it happens,
You'll see it in my ecstasy.

It won't be disguised
When the time comes to fly.

Soaring,
Disregarding the lies—
Both you and I,
We will rise.

If I can,
You can.
The future will stand
Through you and I.

And everyone will know why.

Rise

By Trinity Rucker, City of Rockford's Youth Poet of 2024

Despite the agony and the pain,
I'll rise.

Because a new day has come,
I'll rise.

I'll leave all anger behind,
I won't continue to be blind.

You can't hold me down,
Could never hide me away.

My beauty is precious,
And deserves to be put on display.

Chains have held me for too long,
I'm tired of singing a sorrowful song.

Trials and tribulations won't take my life,
I won't continue to feel anger and strife.

So I'll speak it into existence,
I'll encourage myself.

I'll take the opportunity
And tap into my wealth:

**"I will be set free,
The devil will get off of me.**

**Everything attached to me will win—
The outside,
And within."**

Victory is mine,
And not just this time.

The One to Come

By Trinity Rucker, City of Rockford's Youth Poet of 2024

Looks
And stares,
Glares in return.
Burning buildings,
Fire alarms,
Men's voices that are stern.
Gunshots,
Bodies hit the floor.

Protest,
Protest,
Open the door,
Open it up for the one to come.
Do you know who I am talking about?
Only some.

I speak of the m-e-s-s-i-a-h,
Messiah,
The one who is and is to come,
The Savior.
At His wrath, no one can run.

If you have ears, hear,
Listen when He speaks.

Earth flooded with sin—
There must have been a leak.

Are you on the ship, the one that doesn't sink?
Or "Depart from me, for I never knew you."
Of sin, you reek.

Smiles,
Peace at last.
The world made new,
· Our past wiped away.
Who? Who are you?

Make the choice today—
It could be your last.
Swim in sin,
Or be made new at last.

He Loves You

By Trinity Rucker, City of Rockford's Youth Poet of 2024

When I say
"Jesus loves you,"
I don't want to make you mad.
I just want you to know,
He can wipe away every tear when you're sad.

When I say
"Jesus loves you,"
Know it's true,
That He's there,
No matter what you do.

When I say
"Jesus loves you,"
I don't want to criticize.
I want you to know,
You're beautiful—
Lips, nose, and eyes.

When I say
"Jesus loves you,"
I'm reminding you it's not too late to make it right.

But He could come back this morning,
Afternoon,
Or night.
So,
Jesus loves you,
You see.

He loves you,
Both you and me.

There's no pain He can't take away,
No tear He can't wipe,
Because though you've gone astray,
His love for you is ripe.

Whatever burdens you carry can be thrown away,
Because He carried them for you on the cross that day.

Youth

By Trinity Rucker, City of Rockford's Youth Poet of 2024

You're young,
But never too young that you can't make a change.

You're young,
But never too young you can't amaze.

You're young,
But not to be underestimated,
Because every obstacle that comes your way can be eliminated.

You're young,
But that means more time to figure things out,
More time to let your seed sprout.

You're young,
And that's what a lot of people want to be.
Why?
Because it's our potential that they see.

For it is Written

By Trinity Rucker, City of Rockford's Youth Poet of 2024

For it is written:
I am fearfully and wonderfully made,
For Your love I cannot evade.

There's no place I can go, no mountain I can climb,
To escape Your love,
Because it only grows over time.

It follows me wherever I go—
In the mountains, in the hail, rain, and snow.

"What have I done to deserve Your love?"
Absolutely nothing; it's divine—straight from above.

Jesus wants us to...

Accept the love that He has,
Leave the past in the past.

Accept the love He has for you today,
It's the type of love that never goes away.
The kind that keeps no record of wrongs,
The kind of love that makes you strong.

His love carries no envy or hate,
Only compassion and a clean slate.

Sunrise

By Trinity Rucker, City of Rockford's Youth Poet of 2024

I understand how the world can make you feel.
It can cause pain that feels like no one can heal.
The pain settles down and sinks deep.
Even though it's from the past,
It still lingers and creeps.

Some of us carry sorrowful hearts.
Where can we find rest?
We don't even know where to start.
Feeling lost, looking to the left and to the right,
Desperately searching for something to bring you life.

When you find a speck of joy,
It withers away,
Because it was something everyone else had,
That was temporarily on display.
"When is it my time?"
"Things are so rough."
"What do I do?"
Enough is enough.

Sometimes life can be hard.
Trials and tribulations will give you bruises and scars.

But over time, bruises and scars fade away.
When the sun rises, it's a brand new day.
Pain is a temporary thing,
Joy is everything.

When I feel down,
I look around at all I can see.
I observe: "Life hasn't been… bad to me."
I may have trials, but I have triumphs too.
And now that I think about it, the trials are few.

Every day that I live
Is a new story to give,
And each word that I say
Is a blessing in every way.

Life is what we make it.
We have the power to create.
There's no point in sitting in the background,
Sitting just to speculate.

Don't allow life to pass you by.
It moves so fast.
You never know which day could be your last.
So put your trust in God,
Let Him lead the way.
Let your sun rise,
And embrace a brand new day.

ABOUT THE AUTHOR

Trinity Rucker
at her induction as the
City of Rockford Youth Poet of 2024

Trinity Rucker was born and raised by Pastor Robert and Darlene Rucker in Rockford, IL, under very unusual circumstances. Her parents were well past child-bearing age and defied medical expectations by having an 11-pound baby.

The youngest of six children, she grew up with friends and family at Washington Park Community Center and Maria Montessori School. Her childhood was filled with vacations, singing, dancing, games, family gatherings, movies, music, and her natural gift for reading and mathematics.

Attending her church, The Word Worship Center, Trinity sang, praise danced, and experienced God's goodness at a young age. The older women at the church spoke blessings over her life, even when she couldn't understand them. It was there that she realized she was one of a kind and placed on this Earth for a purpose.

The isolation of 2020 tried to destroy that purpose. All that she had learned—valuing herself, respecting others, and knowing who she was—seemed to slip away.

It was the prayers of her family, especially her parents, that sustained her and eventually brought her out of confusion. The whispering voice of God guided her back to the light.

In sixth grade, her middle school teacher, Ms. Serna, taught about Jacqueline Woodson, an African American writer who captured the trials and triumphs of her people. Woodson's stories encouraged Trinity to create one of her own: a poem called "Years and Years."

Trinity brought the poem to her teacher, not understanding why it brought tears to her eyes. Ms. Serna urged her to allow the poem to be submitted to the Seventh Annual Gwendolyn Brooks Youth Poetry Awards of 2023, and Trinity complied.

In sixth grade, she won an honorable mention, and her poem, "Years and Years," was published in a chapbook alongside the works of other talented writers. The winners gathered in Chicago, IL, at the Reva and David Logan Center for the Arts for the award ceremony.

With her winnings, Trinity was able to spend an entire weekend with her family celebrating. God's favor was on her life; and even when she felt so alone, it never left her.

She went on with her middle school years, joining volleyball and multiple clubs in her after-school program, including Ukuu and Girls on The Move—clubs that empower and teach kids valuable life skills.

Through it all, she continued to write poetry. One day, at Washington Park Community Center, the supervisor, Nikki Lynch, offered to submit Trinity's name into another poetry contest, using two of her poems: "Years and Years" and "The Lord."

At 13 years old, Trinity Rucker became the youngest and first African American City of Rockford Youth Poet in January 2024. The contest was sponsored by the City of Rockford, the Rockford Public Library, and the Rockford Area Arts Council.

For such a small girl, she had huge dreams. The people of her community made those dreams come true with their continuous and unwavering support.

During her term, she used her gift of poetry to educate and inspire people in Rockford, IL. She performed at various banquets, festivals, fundraisers, and other gatherings held at the Coronado, the Nordlof Center (where she hosted her own event, "Speak It, Sing It"), Sinnissippi Park, Levings Lake, Rock Valley College, multiple schools, and the State Fair in Springfield, IL. She has also partnered with many organizations, including Rockford Ready (with whom she created a health literacy commercial) and Nicholas Conservatory, where her poem was featured for their 100th rose garden anniversary.

Trinity is the Vice President and Leader of Fine Arts of the YES Club under the leadership of Carl and Dianna Cole, and the Vice President of the Rockford NAACP Youth Council—both organizations working toward the advancement of the community through peace and unity.

Due to her exposure and tremendous support, Trinity has earned numerous awards and acknowledgments, including the first-ever Winnebago County Chairman's Service Excellence Award, the NAACP "Next Generation" Award, the Live at Levings "You Got Soul" award, acknowledgments from RPS 205 and the Rockford Park District, multiple features in the *Rock River Current*, a page in *Northwest Quarterly* magazine, her own article in *Diamond Affect* magazine, multiple appearances on TV and radio stations, and, due to her exceptional reading and writing skills, the opportunity to spend a week at any college of her choice to explore STEM through the Youth Leadership Forum, among many others.

Trinity's family and community have lifted her to great heights, allowing her to stand before established people—the Mayor, state representatives, business owners, activists, and more. She has formed alliances and friendships that will never fade.

Most importantly, she credits God for all her blessings and acknowledges that if it weren't for Him—her help, her strength, and her peace—she would have lost it all.